Memory Creases

Geoffrey Miller grew up in and around the mining towns of Tasmania's west coast but has lived his adult life in the north-west of the state. The character and culture of these places reflect in both his collections to date: *Behind Closed Eyes* (2010) and now *Memory Creases* (2020), both published by Ginninderra Press.

A chronic stutterer for most of his life, he thought he wrote because it allowed him to express himself freely. Now, with almost total fluency in speaking, he acknowledges he would have written poetry regardless because this is who he is.

Also by Geoffrey Miller and published by Ginninderra Press

Behind Closed Eyes

Geoffrey Miller
Memory Creases

Acknowledgements

To those wonderful people who took my hand and walked me across the perilous gap between loose leaf folders and a completed book, I cheer you.

Dr Kristen Lang for her persistent gentle encouragement and beautiful generous heart, her incisive editing skills and clarity that always nudged me toward a more embraceable image.

Fay Forbes for many years of enthusiastic belief and confidence in me and all who have a heart for writing.

Participants of the Devonport Writers Workshop who provide a welcoming writing family to all who have a story to tell.

And my lifelong friend and wife Elizabeth for her bottomless patients and unshakable support.

For Elizabeth
Your laughing eyes keep dancing
past the windows of my mind

Memory Creases
ISBN 978 1 76041 997 4
Copyright © Geoffrey Miller 2020

First published 2020 by
GINNINDERRA PRESS
PO Box 3461 Port Adelaide 5015
www.ginninderrapress.com.au

Contents

Scattered Treasures
  Adoration   9
  Helpless in the Dark   10
  The Unidentified 'They'   11
  Sleeping Bones   12
  I Didn't Care   13
  Who I Am   14
  Unwilling Captive   15
  Seriously Cynical   16
  Intimate Intrusion   17
  Feeding Time   19
  Recovery   20
  On Reflection   21
  Longing   22
  The Power of Nothing   23
  Embrace Me   25

Dawdling Places
  Living Below the Table   29
  Our Old Orange Tent   31
  A Boat in Mixed Media   33
  The Humming Dunny   34
  Tasmania Smiles   36
  Newness at Dawn   38
  Choosing the Breeze   40
  The Pulse of the Wilderness Sleeps   42
  Wilderness Cherries   43
  Mersey Morning in June   44
  Mt Roland   45
  The Centre   46
  A Lick of Yesterday   47
  Cruising Tropical Waters   49

Unlikely Possibilities

Riding With Santa	53
Spring, Lawns, and Football	54
My Oopses	56
My Magic Mushroom	57
The Musical Fly	58
The Hygiene Glove	60
A Plonk in My Plinker	62
An Obituary for Trevor	63
Counting Cutlery	65
The Ghost of Chocolate	66
Behaviours in Chocolate	67
Role Reversal	69
Trash Dumpsite and Blossom Bloom	72
Mary's Cup of Tea	76

The Present Past

Memory Creases	83
Devonport Community Garden	86
Anzac Day	87
Wednesday Dreaming	89
Undoing a Puzzle	91
Undoing Sudoku	93
A Question For Christmas	95
Be Different	98
Tutankhamun Exhibition: Melbourne	99
Leaving Home	101
Universe, Ants, and Loving God	102
Healing a Promise	104
Fire of Silence	106
Escape	107
Loving and Loathing	108
Black and White Things	110
Late Onset Intelligence	111

Scattered Treasures

Adoration

Your laughing eyes keep dancing
past the windows of my mind
Your golden hair waves
through my sky of time
I live beneath a rainbow
of love you've given me
Within your arms of wonder
I recline.

Helpless in the Dark

Agony twists your face and I tremble,
weakened by the tears
that squeeze from you eyes
and drip off your lip.
Your need calls me
but I'm frozen
locked outside the cell
of your suffering.
Straining through unseen bars
to pull away the black blanket of pain
that covers all but your sobs.
They echo loud now,
between my fear to move
and my longing
to set you free.

In that dark place prayers are real
and I yell that someone
more compassionate than me
can lift one corner of your suffering
so light might enter, and we may see
a haven, floating off heaven's page
and onto yours.
Someone who can open hospital doors
and break through stubborn
waiting lists that separate you from life
and tomorrow's smile.

The Unidentified 'They'

When people play gossip,
'They' is not a collective noun.
Not 'they' like members of a club
who play the same card game
week on week, with cups of tea
and niceties.

Gossip 'They' is a guerrilla fighter,
prowling behind conversations,
ambushing truth. Taunting,
as when a cat cuffs a mouse
and confuses its direction.
Turning its head to a different place.
In that mesmerised state, truth
is guided away to a dozy death.
It has no champion, no one notices
it has gone.

In wrestles of conversation
when stories jostle to speak
and tongues are at full pace,
swarms of 'They say' and 'They reckon'
bounce off walls like flies off windows.
An ambushed victim is stripped
of who they are and presented
as a meal
to the devouring gossips.

Sleeping Bones

When my arthritic bones
recline within sheets
of relief
and sleep bundles them
into a cocoon,
their arguing ceases.
Bone on bone whingeing
stops.

Then I sneak away.

I sneak away to a place
where stiffness, grunt, and grizzle
vaporise in a dream.

And I run.

Beach sand spreading my toes.
My fists buffet the wind.
Crashing waves tumble me.
Salt spray paints my eyes.
I splash water in the face
of the sun.

There is time
to fish,
laugh and love.

Until morning wakes them.

I Didn't Care

When the wind plaited my broad beans
into a green carpet and laid them flat
across the garden path,
as if for a princess to walk upon
and not muddy her shoes,
I didn't care.
I didn't care that my beans had began
a return journey through the compost bin.
Next summer they will come back to me, reborn
as a cauliflower bake with cheese
melted into its heart.
I care only that the princess is you.

I didn't care when the chooks pecked one side
out of every red tomato that I owned.
My tomatoes will come back to me next winter
as a chicken casserole
with onions, peas, and cauliflower bake
dripping cheese.
At my fingertips a bold Coonawarra red,
and certainty
a princess will wander in
to be toasted and adored.
I care only that the toast
welcomes you.

Who I Am

The form said 'Partner'.
I left it blank, because
my heart feels it blank.
'Partner' cannot whisper love to me
the way you do.

'Partner' tells me,
business arrangement.
Return on input.
Fifty-fifty dividends.
With an opt-out option
unwritten
above the door.

If the form had coaxed me
for 'Wife'
or maybe a drab grey 'Spouse',
I would have written
your name
in capitals. Bold Black,
Vibrant Red,
Peaceful Blue,
Compassionate Yellow,
For that is who you are.

Your blending colours
and rolling moods
have washed over me
and changed
who I am.

Unwilling Captive

Dragged protesting from the home I love
by a smiling oppressor.
Wrenched from familiar comforts
and taken to a place
of dark foreboding.

She parades me
in threadbare clothing,
back and forth
through the market place.

She leads me between SALE signs.

My head hangs low, weighing my shoulders
down.

Cords of hopelessness pull me along.
Drips of resentment mark my path.
I am too old to bring a good profit.

Still, merchants with eager eyes
measure and prod me.
Circumference of neck and chest,
inside arm and leg.
Saying 'Yes, this is good.'

My captor nods her approval.

'That will go with your grey trousers
and while I've got you here
you can try on a few jackets.'

Seriously Cynical

For Dad

Politicians make you cynical, son.
You'll agree by the time your days are done.
The flowers that grow on their gilded tongues
are picked by fools and the very young.

No matter how they speak for rights,
they'll never kick the dog that bites.
They pat the heads of wealth and power
and croon 'Puss puss' while dogs devour.

They coax us down a rosy track
with little chance of getting back.
They promise sunshine beyond a hill
they have never climbed, and never will.

Intimate Intrusion

When night brings forth a frisky moon
good friends awake in our bedroom.
They gather round to comfort me
and plan the death of our TV.

These dearest friends I draw upon
are memories from nights now gone.
They take me back and let me see
the dreams we made before TV.

They say to me, 'Recall the blow
when winter howled and threw its snow
across the town and country side.
We were born to your radiant bride.

To each in turn she gave us life
this bed, this room, her love, your life
and nothing ever dared intrude
to break each cherished interlude.

When fire waned from the summer sun
and marching shadows had begun
across the bed toward the door
you mined a very precious ore,

and from it cast a golden glove
that held the radiance of your love.
There we made another friend
and toasted loves most potent blend.

We drank to blonde hair over breasts
while almost silent whispers stressed
advancing love without retreat
where no TV should dare compete.

TV is pretence and nothing more.
An image of what's gone before.
An image born in someone's head
who has no place beside your bed.'

My friends of years all gather round,
to bring this cruel intrusion down.
To bring retreat upon its head
and leave us quiet within our bed.

But it stands cold against the wall.
Without love's tingles to recall.
Without desire and cheeky play.
My sadness weeps.
    It's here to stay.

Feeding Time

In autumn
aboard a jet
rising
into a red
dawn
I can see
snakes of fog
whiting out
traffic
from freeways,
and sun splashes
on ridges
where giant
mortgages
wake
for feeding.

Recovery

They took your knee
and gave you back to me
bent
like a child baulking
at its first step
its arms reaching
for the world.

On Reflection

The light of living
shines on me
as it chooses,
not as I want,
how, or when.

It comes like the sun,
in its own time,
strobing through the twisting
of my day.

Spotlighting the fragility
of a smile
that restrains an angry snap,
melting it away
before it can become
who I am.

So part of me grows,
part of me dies, and anyone
who bounces against me
can walk away
without bruises.

Longing

Longing is a child's kite
black against the sky.
Dancing on a cord of desire.
Rolling upward to hope.
Hissing downward to destruction.
A wrestle between the anchored
and the free.

The Power of Nothing

'Because there is a law such as gravity,
the Universe can and will create itself from nothing.'
– Professor Stephen Hawking

Nothing is wonderful stuff.
It grows. Slowly, of course,
because nothing has no need to hurry.

It grows into a celestial clock
that ticks its way around itself.
Then into a mind that measures the ticking
and tells the time.
And to carry the mind on its journey
between the hours,
legs and feet,
that rest at night, crossed in front of the fire.

A fire that flares from a tree
that grew in the mountains
years ago.
It was a giant that drew its breath
from the hills and drank from the stream
that washed the bank, winter by winter,
until the roots were bare.
It fell,
evicting a family of ringtails
and bridging the creek.

Now its molecules crackle and spit, spent nothing
up the chimney
and back to the Great Emptiness
that wears the universe on its wrist.
That made a Labrador to lay across my feet
while I doze,
my book collapsed in my lap
and my mind
floating off to nowhere,
embraced by nothing.

Embrace Me

I am a poem
on a page,
stalled on the journey
from
heart to mind.
Wake me.
Shake me.

I need eyes to raise me.
Without thought
I cannot stir.
Stroke me.
Poke me.

I can dance.
I sing.
Wrestle chance.
Welcome spring.
Crumple sheets on a winter's night.
Laugh joy in the face of fright.

But not without you.

You can fly me to places
my heart wants to go.
Splash in my puddles.
Roll in my snow.

Shake me
Wake me
Take me away
Don't leave me sleeping
at the door of your day.

Embrace me.
I am a poem.

Dawdling Places

Living Below the Table

When our octopusical family
comes together in its generations
all tentacles lead back
to the kitchen table.
There, noise buries everything.
Brag contests brag.
Beer lubricates lies.
Fish pile up in imaginations.
Light rods and hair thin lines
land threshing monsters.

Ninety-metre goals
kicked into a howling gale
become the measure.
Bats and balls smoke
with the telling
of centuries before lunch.

Among the rattling buckets
of verbal extravagance
ladies exchange recipes
and make fifty pounds of chutney
in a day.

Beanies for African babies
appear in pearl and plain, from
multicoloured wool
unravelled from dead jumpers
and triumphant op shop finds.

Below the table, below
the blustering winds
of verbiage and crashing waves
of brinkmanship,
our toes, yours and mine,
reach for each other, touch
and embrace, dancing together
in a slow sway.
Smiles float between us
carrying a wink.
And without embellishment,
everything we could say
is said.

Our Old Orange Tent

She's been lumped to Cradle Mountain
more than her share of times.
She's done the plod up Pelion Pass
and other heart break climbs.
She's sat among the puddles
when the fog fell on Frog Flats.
The morning sun on Ossa's face,
she could tell of that.

She turned a night of mountain rain
the first time she went out.
Though water pooled beneath the floor
we were drier than a drought.
She's heard wild wombats rustle
in the blackness of the night
and heard the devils growling
as fight gave way to flight.

Bush mice scampering through the grass,
the thump of kangaroos,
and possum piss upon the roof:
she could tell that story too.
She's wandered through Tasmania's wilds
and slept by mountain lakes,
and even spent a night or two
where rolling oceans break.

But she didn't need a wilderness
with granite peaks to roam.
She rested happy on the lawn
set up right at home.
There she spent her summer days
sagging in the sun.
Pushed and shoved by wrestling kids
and reaping scars of fun.

She's not a polished high-tech girl
with fancy carbon rods.
She'd never stand an arctic blow,
she's just a Kmart job.
But though she's looking faded
and though she's looking old
her life is quite a story
and a story to be told.

A Boat in Mixed Media

Devonport Art Gallery

Three spark plugs. One English, two Canadian,
all dead. The hull red. And a propeller
that kids spin with fingers.
Fun art, moored to the gallery wall.

A reason to stop, smile, wonder
if the little boat with abstract
personality
could navigate the reefs and oceans
of my mind.

That place of sunshine and clouds
where jagged surprises
lie inches below
the surface of a smile.
Where a sudden wave can break
over the stern
and swirl laughter away
from a quiet drink on a calm day.

Could it navigate
the shifting pressures
that roll behind my eyes, building a storm
so fierce the tiller
would turn and run for shelter
in a place less real.

Days like those, I could pray to these spark plugs
and believe that they live.

The Humming Dunny

I can hear the dunny humming
in the sultry summer sun
when I push the slab door open
and the bush flies rise as one.

A skinky lizard scampers
through the crack along the floor.
A wad of paper dangles
from the nail behind the door.

Locked in that box of dimness
I can hear cicadas call.
And play with shafts of sunlight
through the rust holes in the wall.

I feel a sweat bead trickle
down my belly in the heat.
And run to tell my mother
someone piddled on the seat.

That dunny's quietly rusting
in the backyard of my years.
Sometimes I need to go there
to relieve the weight of fears.

I sit among my cobwebs
and the droning of life's flies.
I can hear my mother singing.
I can hear the baby cry.

I can hear my father calling
in his rough old bushman's way,
'Are you in there, little cobber'
and I know the world's OK.

Tasmania Smiles

I've watched the heavy surf pound in,
felt the spray and heard the din.
Laughed as bothered sea gulls squawked,
and scurried sideways, as I walked
among the cast up shells and weed
and never felt alone.
For out of the mist and tumbling sea
Tasmania rose and smiled at me.

At times I've sat on weathered stones
and shared her lofty alpine home
where tarns and pencil pines are friends.
Button grasses sway and bend
to the southern breath of the mountain wind
that bears the kiss of snow.
A refreshing kiss from a gentle soul
whose living makes my being whole.

And too, I've fished a rural creek
where platypus play hide and seek.
Rocky ripples bubble by.
Blackwoods gently creak and sigh
and cast a pool of picnic shade
where dozing cattle lay.
There she sang by summer bees.
Swept me up and smiled at me.

And when she smiles I'm fully whole,
I can't begrudge the heart she stole.
Nor could I think there is a price
I wouldn't pay with sheer delight
to be seduced for all my days,
by her beauty and her easy ways.
I'm free from care and life's debris
every time she smiles at me.

Newness at Dawn

At dawn
when birds negotiate softly
on their way
to their morning arguments,
and the sun
rustles the curtains
just enough
to disturb the blackness
and tip
a shadow from the shelf.

In that between time;
between yesterday
and today.

Your soft hand glides
across my belly folds
awakening dreams.
Shiraz and Edam,
on twilit nights, by the pond.
When we talked, without words.

Gliding down the back
of my arm
you lock tiny fingers
between mine, and squeeze.

Gentle breathing
whispers a lifetime.
Each finger for a decade.
A whole hand for the history
of being locked together.
Unwilling to move lest it break
the newness beginning.

Choosing the Breeze

8:45 a.m.
    In the City Mall.
        Power People scamper
            past my nose. Past my
                takeaway coffee, and vanish
                    into their mortgages.

Black and grey suits
    and skirts shout action.
        'Don't hesitate', 'Seize the day'
            'What time is it?'
                'Damn the bus.'

Pull-along files click over tiles.
    Sensible heels tap rhythms.
        They race to a beginning,
           to prepare an end
                for kids who went to bed
                    unchuckled.

When the post office clock
              yawns
a lazy nine
    they are gone.

A blonde woman in a red dress that loves her
and will remember her long after she has hung it out to dry
floats by.

A family of tourists play tug-o'-war with a map
and argue
for the movies or the museum.

My coffee cup runs off with the breeze,

        and I follow.

The Pulse of the Wilderness Sleeps

Tourist disappointment floods across the tracks,
rusting the rails and soaking sleepers in sorrow.
They whispered along the station platform
and through the cafeteria: 'It's not the same.'
'The pulse has gone from the wilderness.'
Its rhythms locked away in a rusty shed
with the shiny green loco
that hisses, puffs and sways along the torture
of the King River Gorge,
that lays morning mist of smoke and steam
over man ferns, moss and myrtle, like a blanket
around the shoulders of an old friend.
The little train that clunks the wilderness awake
and makes it live in modern eyes.

Just for today a diesel purrs,
free from the rolling steam and acrid smoke
that can pull a hundred years
across a trestle bridge, along ravines,
and up inclines that can't hold a stop sign
to hissing history.
Today we purr through rainforest,
but the pulse of the wilderness sleeps in the shed
with its little green friend.

Wilderness Cherries

Cherries on the train.
Spitting pips at King River. Both of us
introduced.

Mersey Morning in June

Fingers of frost hold the river
still, like a mirror
for morning to pretty her face.

The sun yawns somewhere below the sky
and night withdraws to crimson.

Ice fairies blink on grass tips, and a possum
comes home from a party.

Gulls fly seaward skimming silence,
images reflecting belly to belly.

Beacons throw ribbons, red and green
that unroll and vanish
on a shingled shoal.

A fisherman's jetty, charcoal etched,
huddles a brood of riggings,
tangled black to black.

In the shallows, water clings to polished stones
Like fruit jelly refrigerated
for a child's picnic.

Morning lays a cold kiss upon my cheek.
And when my eyes close in summer
it is still there.

Mt Roland

Her majesty the mountain
so regally attired.
No genius of the fashion world
was ever so inspired.
Snow bonnet of the purest white
trimmed round with crocheted lace
sits dominant upon her head
and frames her ancient face.

Her bodice, cut in granite blue
gathered in dark folds.
Stitched by nature's patient hands
with wind and rain and cold.
Within the folds as they fall
ravines in shadowed shades
that catch the mist that trickles down
through rock and mossy glades.

The skirt she wears defies compare
with any movie queen,
appliquéd in towering gums
of mottled olive green.
Falling full around her feet,
her undulating hills,
and hemmed around the border,
a stream, so quiet and still.

The Centre

Where Yin and Yang
hang
suspended.
Balancing nothing
worth drinking over.
Mooded faces
neither welcomed
nor opposed.

At the centre,
there are no belly laughs.
No tear-soaked shirts.
No reason to hug
or withdraw.
No differences
to cherish.

A Lick of Yesterday

I lick the mixing spoon like a child,
sweeping around the Tupperware bowl
in a preschool trance,
chasing down every titbit,
savouring deliciousness.
My seventy-year-old smile
calling out my childhood
with every slurp.

I feel the weight of porcelain
and remember crow feet cracks
meandering through glaze.
A forgotten maker fired his mark
into the clay about the time
my parents married.

A stainless steel mixing spoon
is wooden warm in my hand.
Its twisted handle reaches above my shoulder
and brushes past my hair.

It is the spoon my grandfather carved
from a sassafras limb
when he cleared the farm.
The one that stirred lamingtons,
jam and date puddings.
The one that bruised backsides
and watered eyes when boys forget
they were boys.

When the bowl, spoon, and dreams
are licked clean, I hold them tight
unwilling to return to my arthritis.

Cruising Tropical Waters

Decks stacked, pancake like and blinding white,
loaded to the plimsoll line with exotic promises.

Junkish 'duty free' sparkles a bigger dream
and hidden whispers to buy more
keep it all afloat.

Polished waves fracture beneath the bow
and surface again, tumbling from the stern,
the scar stretching back to the horizon.

Warm breezes shuffle through the hair
of the on-deck rock band, blasting out
superannuation for audiologists.

Each island rises up, scripted by Disney, with a palm
hairdo and a necklace of breaking foam.

We return their greeting – the thunderous
dancing of anchor chains.

A circular rolling of tender boats,
ship to shore, and four thousand feet
stomping across the beauty.

They welcome us with village drums, their songs
hidden in dialect, telling stories (I think) of the gawking
mesmerised, washed up from beyond the clouds.

Children, giggling smiles, feign shyness. Delightful posers
In uncluttered time, splashing in the lagoon,
wrestling in the sand, how they'll still

be there after tourists have sailed away,
the cruise drifting into the next 'best thing'.

My watch whispers: last tender boat and I slop
and roll back into place amid the excess – choreographed,
every whim picked up and polished to a purr.

The waiter, production line perfect, welcomes me
as if he has known me from school, floats a napkin
across my knees, ticks off the menu in perfect French.

I order a mystery that comes with a compliment of
'wise choice' and a side of never-knowing-what-it-was.

Fifteen days of sun falling off the horizon
and clambering back on the other side. Fifteen days
of bartering for coconuts

painted with ugly faces, polished shells
with the dust capacity of a bucket. Fifteen

days and I want to be real again.
Mow a lawn, plant some spuds, hug a child, become
useful.

Unlikely Possibilities

Riding With Santa

Crashing through the creek,
an esky by his side,
Santa came to our house
to take me for a ride.
He wanted someone who
was true blue and knew
how to pour a cold beer
while he had things to do.
He took me flying free
up into the sky.
I served him refreshments
whenever he got dry.
One for the elf and for myself.
The reindeers all drank wine.
We missed a lot of presents
but we had a lovely time.

Spring, Lawns, and Football

I'm not in love with springtime; it brings no joy to me.
I'm not moved by soothing sun nor hovering honey bees.
I see lawns up to my nose, or at least up to my knees,
and footy finals come round then to scintillate and tease.

It's not my fault if springtime comes when footy's at its height.
When grass is growing through the fence and the yard's a frightful sight.
Mother buys some mower fuel and plonks it by the door,
then tells me that the lawn's the likes she's never seen before.

And it's true the grass has grown to about a goalpost high.
But I'm tucked up with the goggle box where the mighty big men fly.
The Cats and Blues and Magpies too entrance me mummified.
I'm not ashamed to love the game – that's never been denied.

Now if perchance some circumstance should roll me from my chair,
to tiptoe past the arctic blast and chilling, drilling stare,
I disregard her commentary and dwell upon the play,
for years of springtime football has taught me what she'll say:

'Hail! His mighty majesty is finally off his bum.
The hand of God is on him, the resurrection's come.
He'll take our creeping jungle yard and turn it to a park.
I'll mix him up a nice cool drink and he can work away till dark.'

Unsinged by the fearsome fires of hell, I shuffle to the loo.
I'll grab a stubby coming back, better make that two.
Ten points down in the final term, but the game can still be won.
And she calls this great intensity, sitting on your bum.

Now I'm not a bloke who doesn't try to think the problem through,
I ponder it at quarter time and through the long break too.
I'm not one to go and say that God has got it wrong,
but why does springtime come around when footy finals are on?

My Oopses

My oopses come in many forms, usually they're within the norm –
I spill the tea or burn the toast, these are the oopses I do most.

I've often failed to feed the dog. I overstayed the house of grog
and heard the magistrate decide that I should walk instead of ride
and in his very solemn looks discerned – that really was a nasty oops.

One winter night in pouring rain impatient to be home again
I stooped to see the ignition key locked in the car where I should be.
I kicked the car until it shook – that was misery's cruellest oops.

Sweet Melanie was full of fun; she also had the cutest bum,
and other bits were lovely too; we dawdled through the evening dew
to places we had never been. *We called that little oops Darlene.*

We planned an anniversary date but I forgot and worked till late.
When my memory clog unblocked I found the florist dark and locked.
That night I entertained the chooks. *That was not a happy oops.*

I think of all the oopse I've done and contemplate the oopses to come
and wonder if some oopses might be the catastrophic end of me.

I might decide that God's a joke and not the bloke the scriptures quote.
I might decide that flesh and blood crawled out of some primeval mud,
then die and find God's not kaput. *Now that's a 'What a bugger oops.'*

Until then I'll oops along, I'll mumble oops when things go wrong
and if my memory lets me down and I forget the wife in tow – *Oooooops!*

My Magic Mushroom

I had a mate drop in to see me a month or two ago.
He was kind of all excited and he said I ought to know
that he'd got onto a fungus that you brewed up in a pot
and it made you really healthy whether you were crook or not.

Now I'm a bloke who goes for broke, I've shed some skin and tears
and reaped a swag of aches and pains that plagued me through the years.
'Can't hurt at all,' me old mate said, 'to give this stuff a go.'
'Good health's the aim so join the game or else you'll never know.'

So he turns up with a mushroom and he shows me what to do.
Within about a week or so I had this little brew
that smelt a bit like vinegar and tasted much the same.
'What the hell,' my mad side said. 'Guts it if you're game.'

It bit me like a bull ant and my mouth and throat went numb.
I felt my eyes cross over and both hands gripped my bum.
If this was nature's healing, it must be hell to die.
Bright lights flashed all around me. My whole life passed me by.

But Persevere's my second name and I would not be beat.
It wasn't long before I took my fungal heart start neat.
And sure enough my aches and pains and ringing ears were gone
and I foresaw my wrinkled youth just going on and on.

My good wife of some forty years grew pleasing to my eye.
A wave of warmth washed over me each time that she passed by.
My advances grew persistent and she resisted hard.
My mushroom, brew, and bottle too, she buried in the yard.

The Musical Fly

On a cold and bleak rundown street
a composer worked but didn't eat.
The melody just wouldn't come.
Days went by but no work was done.

To his studio came a young fly
with a marvellous musical eye.
It walked on the manuscript sheets,
making musical notes with its feet.

The spotting had classical flair,
the lilting style quite debonair.
Maestro saw gold in each note
and put his name to all the fly wrote.

He grew richer than he'd ever dreamed
and bathed in great fame and esteem.
He was no longer painfully poor
nor living in filth like before.

A chambermaid came in to clean.
The studio sparkled and gleamed.
No scraps laid decayed on the sink.
No half eaten meat pies to stink.

The fly found no grime for its feet,
Without scraps it had nothing to eat.
It starved and fell dead to the floor,
was swept with the dust out the door.

With no music written each day,
no new compositions to play,
the maestro soon dwindled from fame.
Now no one remembers his name.

The Hygiene Glove

Each time we buy a lunch or snack
and watch that hygiene glove attack
some shredded lettuce or a roll
or grab a leg of chicken whole
or stack a sandwich bit by bit
and swirl a twirl of salt on it,
we know for sure we've felt the love
of our dear friend, the hygiene glove.

The hygiene glove protects us from
all kinds of nasties that might bomb
our bowel and twisting inner parts
and make us so afraid to fart
we close our eyes and screw our face,
scared that some lukewarm disgrace
should trickle down from up above.
So we praise that hygiene glove.

It takes the money, wipes the bench.
Gives the garbage lid a wrench.
Grabs a cold can from the fridge.
Cracks a stubbie from its lid.
Flicks wet hair out of the eyes.
Removes a cup, backhands a fly.
All this is done so we might be
attended to hygienically.

So if we come to greet the day
our body fluids drain away
and lock us tightly to a seat
because some bug has stamped its feet
and shook a fist as lunch went by,
so joy becomes our wish to die.
At least we'll know, for we have seen,
the hand within the glove…was clean

A Plonk in My Plinker

There's a plonk in my plinker
as you can tell
when I press for a plink
it's plonking as well.

I've recently oiled it
and renewed the bell
but it's no longer casting
that sweet angel's spell.

How I long for a plink
that is so crystal clear
that it falls like a spell
on the listening ear

and rolls like the song
of a bird on a bow.
I wish I could fix it
but I don't know how.

An Obituary for Trevor

Old Trevor was a happy bloke
full of chat and cheer
who loved a conversation
and a willing friendly ear.

He had a mind for detail.
A memory so keen
that stories bubbled out
like a rushing mountain stream.

He'd prop himself against a wall
and wave his arms around
to emphasise some strange event
that happened in the town.

You'd never say, 'Hello, old mate.'
You'd never say, 'G'day.'
Old Trev would lock you to the spot
and you'd be there to stay.

He could tell the weather forecast
three months in advance.
Which teams would win, and all the teams
that never had a chance.

He could tell you to the minute
why the mayor was such a fool.
Why his grandkids were all champions
and geniuses in school.

Few men have earned such deep respect,
freely given and complete.
When Trevor took a stroll through town
they gave him half the street.

Now Trevor's gone and memories long
are written on each face
with a subtle hint of happiness
and not a wet eye in the place.

Counting Cutlery

There was an ornate silver knife
and a sparkling silver fork,
they often met at dinner
but they never paused to talk.
They never shared the wittiness
and niceties of love.
They never kissed and giggled
behind the gravy jug.

One evening as the candelabra
twinkled on the glass
they softly brushed together
as the broccoli passed,
they felt a funny feeling
they had never felt before,
now there's twenty little spoons
in the cutlery drawer.

The Ghost of Chocolate

It has no legs but it walks.

Out of the fridge. Out of the glove box.
Out of my undies drawer.
I know it has passed by for I see it
smiling on family faces.

It has no tongue but it talks.

Whispering beyond my hearing.
Calling everyone, but me.
Across the ads on TV.

It guides them away to places
where smugness is smudged on faces.
Licked away with a sigh
and passing by, I know.

I know, it has called to them.

Behaviours in Chocolate

If you're a chocolate lover
And you're looking for another
To share delightful moments
With soft centres and nougat
If you long for eyes that twinkle
As you shake a chocolate sprinkle
On your coffee or your ice cream
With your moistened lips ajar

Then the fella you are seeking
Is not the bloke that's speaking
When it comes to chocolate eating
I prefer to eat alone
In the succulence of munching
With the nuts and raisins crunching
I can cast the savage shadow
Of a mongrel with a bone

My chocolates are not for sharing
Oohing aahing and comparing
Those softly blended flavours
That make drunken senses sway
If anyone comes near me
They should tip toe by and fear me
For I'll bare my teeth and threaten
Until they haste away

But, but…

Should I find my store diminished
And my crumpled wrappers finished
And thrown upon the table
Like a midden by the shore
And you should come to visit
With some dairy blend exquisite
I'll declare you are my dearest precious
Friend forever more.

Role Reversal

I heard them chewing wisdom on the local ABC
and the fragrance of philosophy came drifting over me.
They said that men and women could live their lives in peace.
If they practised role reversal – strife and pain would cease.

I must admit I did not hear the half of what they said.
They were nearly finished when a light shone in my head.
None the less I heard enough to know that I could be
the perfect application of male sensitivity.

I pondered role reversal for at least a week or more.
How should I begin it? Well, I wasn't really sure.
I'm not a bloke that rushes in and knocks the world apart,
I tend to ponder long and hard before I make a start.

Should I reverse the hand towel or the glad wrap in the drawer?
Or perhaps the roll of garbage bags out on the laundry floor.
I rejected sticking plaster as the hardest roll to do
and decided to reverse the roll that hangs out in the loo.

Nothing really happened when I turned the roll around.
No angels started singing, no stars came floating down.
The purpose of the exercise seemed rather vague to me.
I thought this must be something where I had to wait and see.

Some little time had passed before my sweetie said to me.
'Did you reverse that toilet roll out in the lavatory?'
'Why yes, my dearest one,' I said, 'and though it may seem strange,
I think there's other rolls round here that should be rearranged.'

She took that long and silent breath that tells me there's a tack
that I have stuck in her backside and she's sending several back.
Her lip turned down upon her chin, her eyes rolled to the sky.
I felt the wind and rattle of a lecture passing by.

'A toilet roll is not a game, it's not out there for fun.
There is a right and proper way a toilet roll is hung.
The flap goes down against the wall in a neat and tidy way,
not dangling wrinkled down the front like a flasher on display.'

I lost a bit in confidence and baulked I must admit.
One part of me said persevere another part said quit.
Should we strive to roll reverse or live our lives the same?
Then like a mad addicted fool I turned that roll again.

A moaning sound out in the loo ascended to a roar.
The seat slapped down, the cistern flushed, slamming shook the door.
Then like a rabid starving bear bursting from its cave,
a toilet roll hung in her hand, her eyes a fury blaze.

The rules for fixing toilet rolls rotated through my head.
I felt a wild foreboding fear, and she was seeing red.
I backed away with eyes turned down to pacify this strife.
Then turned and bolted through the door, chased by her advice.

Now, I live in a caravan beside a scrubby creek.
The measure of tranquillity defies the words I speak.
The breeze that rustles tree to tree, the giggling creek at dawn.
Cattle lowing on the hill, my fifty-acre lawn.

My toilet roll hangs back to front, there is no right way round.
The floppy bit comes to the front and dangles limply down.
And even though our changing rolls bought forth some nasty hurts,
I can only say in retrospect that roll reversal works.

Trash Dumpsite and Blossom Bloom

(a romance)

Trash Dumpsite wore his crumpled hat
cocked sideways on his head,
summer flies cruised round him
and he smelt like he was dead.

He spent his winters trapping
in the hills behind St Claire.
No soap had soothed his crusty skin
nor foamed his tangled hair.

His heart was set on courting,
on dreams of house and home,
so dreary tired of lonely nights
out in the bush alone.

All winter long his heart had pined
for youthful Blossom Bloom.
He knew she quietly loved him
for when he passed she'd swoon.

Both hands would clasp her bosom
and she gasped a fading sigh
that dwindled to a gurgle
each time that he passed by.

The memory of her glassy eyes,
her blank hypnotic stare,
confirmed that he might claim her
if only he would dare.

He whistled down the pathway
toward sweet Blossom's place,
anticipation spread a glow
across his rugged face.

A bunch of wilting flowers
hung limply in his hand
and spoke a silent message
of a sentimental man.

He rattled on the fly screen.
The watchdog slunk away.
His heart rehearsed the tender verse
his lips were meant to say.

The door came partly open
and the face that filled his dreams
went winter white and filled the night
with horror-curdled screams.

She rushed inside and grabbed the phone
and quickly dialled her mum.
The silent stalking odour
left no safe place to run.

She felt her head grow dizzy,
her countenance grow pale,
but mothers have solutions
and mothers never fail.

'Well,' said Mum, 'it seems to me
this bloke's from outer space.
Old Granny told me years ago
they hang around our place.

She said they're rough and scruffy
and the surest way to tell
is they wear a filthy crumpled hat
and ooze an awful smell.'

'That's him,' Blossom blurted out.
'Mum! Tell me what to do.'
'Listen carefully, Bloss,' she said,
to what I'm telling you.

By the sink on the second shelf
where your father kept his teeth,
you'll find an old spray bottle
that will bring the brute to grief.

I've never actually seen it work
but I heard Old Granny say
if you spray them twice with Soaptynite
they simply melt away.'

She grabbed the old spray bottle
and she bolted to the door.
With pistol-packing pumping,
she gave him three or four.

The rapid-acting Soaptynite
cut through the powerful pong.
Drip by drip the dirt fell off
till everything was gone.

He stood there in his birthday suit
as bright as angel white.
Sweet Blossom cast a searching eye
and said, 'Eh! You're all right!'

Now in the hills behind St Claire,
when the winter snows lay deep,
when the kero lamps are turned down low
and the kids are fast asleep,

when Trash has pegged his possums out
and skun his final roo,
Blossom takes a big deep breath
and whispers, 'I love phewwww.'

Mary's Cup of Tea

(an obituary)

It's sorrowful that I relate
the death of Mary Weathergate,
who left this earth to meet again
the men with whom she shared a name.

For Mary married many men,
folklore says as much as ten,
others guess at six or more.
Truth it is she married four.

Boston Bun was number one,
he was the baker's only son.
Not long after they were wed
poor Boston found his father dead.

Boston fraught with mourning grief
found in Mary warm relief
and she, to make his sorrow flee,
made him many cups of tea.

Porcelains most gentle clink
would indicate a coming drink
of Mary's most delicious brew
to bring dear Boston life anew.

But sad to say it could not be,
in spite of Mary's cups of tea,
Boston slipped away from pain,
setting sorrow free to reign.

Secondly she married Mel.
He owned the Bawdy Bitch Hotel.
Their businesses became combined
the same way that their lives entwined.

Sweet Mary gave her life to Mel
and with her beauty cast a spell
that set his spirit soaring free,
refreshed by many cups of tea.

But sorrow could not wait to laugh
and threw a shadow down their path.
The face of Mel grew ashen grey
and from her love hold slipped away.

Ashgrove Brea was number three,
a businessman from Mersey Lea.
His Mary said, 'What joy to see
a man who loves his cup of tea.'

Mary's eyes could smile again.
The tears that fell like summer rain
became the smile that dressed her lips
while brewing pots of Tiny Tips.

Ashgrove was a man of strength,
who went to well considered lengths
to tend his health and merry mirth
but winter took him from the earth.

Mary wailed and howled her grief
and cursed at death the heartless thief.
She railed at God to why he would
condemn her still to widowhood.

Mary walked through fifty's door
before she married number four,
the older Rupert Weathergate,
a man of rather large estate.

A wealthy man who'd never wed
nor led a woman to his bed,
nor felt a soft leg part his knees,
nor woke to morning cups of tea.

Mary changed his solemn life
and made him wish he'd met his wife
when he was young and washed with health
instead of chasing lonely wealth.

But still he felt a warming glow
of satisfaction just to know
his moneybag was not alone,
wed to wealth to match his own.

But then the gods of fortune frowned.
The corners of their lips turned down.
Mary woke to find him dead.
An empty cup beside the bed.

Now Mary's gone to that place far
where all her long dead lovers are
and there's no doubt they'll turn and flee
should she suggest a cup of tea.

The Present Past

Memory Creases

Rain fell in San Francisco, sweeping Union Square.
Washing us under a veranda
beside a bus stop
to wait
for a gap in the splatter.
And for the walk
to a warm hotel
and coffee.

She waited too, the grey woman.
Grey hair, grey skin,
grey coat, ankle length,
wound tight
around skinny ribs.
Flashes of headlight-lit creases
that ran snake-like,
width and breadth,
through weary fabric.
One for every doorway
she had slept in.
One for every rainy night
she shivered herself awake.
A crease for every memory.
She waited, like she knew how.

He came from nowhere,
as if the night opened
and he fell out.
Business written across his hat.
Finance badged into his suit.
Shoes shone a shine man's dollar.
His briefcase held confidence
and perhaps
crumbs of an eco-friendly
lunch.

He stopped a metre from her face.
Eye to eye
with nothing to say.
No words, no nod.
Strangers in a common place.
A cigarette appeared between his fingers,
lifted to her mouth, parting her lips.
She breathed his held out flame.
Lifting her shoulders, spreading her chest.
Until she was alive again.

He turned to the bus, the door hissed.
He was gone.
Swallowed by the night that spewed him out.

She drew hard, the tip glowed,
faded and glowed.
Each puff leaving a layer of life on her bones.
Making her strong.
She seemed a little taller.

Shuffling onto the street.
Treading over rainbow reflections
that dance on wet bitumen.
To another doorway
on the down side of the wind.
To press one more memory
into the creases of her coat.

We sat in a warm lounge
sipping coffee still tied
to that bus stop.
Their flame-lit faces pressing creases
that shiver from her doorway
to ours.

Devonport Community Garden

Tucked in a corner of town,
mostly unseen.
Locals come and go
most don't know
the beauty they almost touched.
Behind the hedge, earth breaks open,
pushing up new life;
smiled on by those who wait
and anticipate
the wonder of living dirt.
Compost and chipper unite
as a green team,
blending life with death,
giving breath
to colours that reach up
to be held.
The rainbow Fairy Garden
laughs as children play.
The kids laugh too.
Fairies are true.
Even grandparents believe.

Anzac Day

They were gone when I went past,
those old bones, dragged from their beds
to meet lost mates before the dawn.

The breeze off the river bit my face.
Cold watered my eyes
as pain had watered theirs.

The cenotaph stood as stubborn
as the old heads that had bowed
before it.

Limp flags hung at half mast,
the flag of Australia and Union Jack.
Together but separate,
and proud to be.

The torment of war lay heavy.

I felt their mates in the shadows.
The spirits called home
by a bugler's prayer.

Leaving their jungle graves
they jostled each other,
laughing in silence.

Larrikins of the Somme, Kokoda, Korea.
Nurses of the Pacific, untouched
by the guns that felled them.

From out of the sea they had risen.
Desert graves broke open.
Jungle barbed wire lay down for them.

They had come home for the day,
longing to touch the jewel
they had left in our care.

Wednesday Dreaming

Wednesday wears the face
of a lonely man sitting
on a cold stone of hope.
Wedged between future
and past.
Longing for last weekend
reaching for next.
Owning neither.

Wednesday lusts again
for body contours. Moulded
against each other.
His floating hand
soft along her spine.
Gently stretched elastic,
smiling sighs.
Searching lips on a warm neck
whispering toward a bedroom door
yet to be opened.

Wednesday dreams that past delights
will live again in the soft beat
of future nights.
A cover band strumming in
a corner.
A close foxtrot on a half lit square
and just enough wine to stir
possibilities into soft hair.

He shuffles between dreams,
her perfume pulling both ways.
Back to a fading vapour,
forward to throbbing fancy,
with no path to the past
and the future too far away.

Undoing a Puzzle

She was a crossword
that challenged.
Mingling common and complex
in playful mischief.
She offered more clues than answers.
Her thoughts hidden in youthful bubbles
that floated on possibilities.

There were mysteries to reveal,
new words to form,
as she laughed each year
into womanhood.

She thought his words of love
filled the same spaces hers did.

He thought she was lucky
he came by when she needed him
and craved her body
without knowing
she was a mind to coax
beautiful answers from.

Slowly

he bent her lines into circles
that kept bringing her back
to something easier.
A nod for an opinion.
A sigh for a thought.

He blacked out squares
that needed a letter.
He wrote his words
that pushed her off the page.
Down and across never mingled again.

They haven't had an argument
in years.

Undoing Sudoku

He was a Sudoku
completed by his father
before he was old enough
to count to nine.
The older voice chasing down
every combination his young heart
reached for.

There were no mysteries to unravel.
No patterns to reveal.
Shouldering each square, he carried
his bruises into manhood.

He thought her words of love
filled the same spaces his did.

She thought he was lucky
she had found in him his good heart.
She would shuffle his numbers,
reverse his duplications,
balance his patterns.
Coaxing him out of his jumble.

Slowly

she became blind to his own
inverted nines.
His horizontal threes
she once thought were funny
now bent blank in her sigh.

He drew back to darker squares,
hidden from her scowl.
She stopped rocking numbers
locked down in a father's
stubborn frown.

They haven't laughed together
In years.

A Question For Christmas

Why didn't you tell me
life was up for grabs?
That a little helpless child
could lift a massive slab
of thoughtlessness and fractured hope,
that He alone could break the rope
that bound me to a selfish me,
so I could stand and wander free,
to love without the need to win.
That a different heart can begin
to live and move and feel the need
of the homeless, oppressed and refugee.
That I can walk within their shoes
and be their voices when there're accused.

Why didn't you tell me
that a different heart
in a manger laid
can shape the breadth of every day
and break the sound of an inner voice
that can't embrace the risky choice
to love, and share, and just be there,
when no one else will love or care?
That voice that thinks the world begins
at the point on earth where my toes dig in.

Why didn't you tell me?
That a bridge across the grave
was built in a baby's cry.
That God so loved this ditsy world
He could not pass it by
and leave it in its hopelessness,
defeated every day by death.
The story you tell is not the one
of a helpless child and a victory won.
That death has lost its vicious sting.
This is why the angels sing.

You told me they sing a spending spree,
tinsel, toys, and the GDP.
That they sing a day of gifts and fun,
barbecues and cold beer in the sun.
That they sing small kids with sparkling eyes
wrestling with some giant surprise
that tips them almost upside down,
and keeps the economy spinning round.

The baby sleeps in the manger still.
The shepherds sit up in the hills.
And twiddle their thumbs, no tale to tell.
The wise men shrug and say, 'Oh well,
let's go home. There's nothing to see
but a bulging fridge and a Christmas tree.'
'Loved the lights and the pulsing stars,
but don't know why we came so far.
Have no idea why we were sent
or where the king of new life went.'

But the baby sleeps in the manger still,
unstirred by the rowdy Christmas trill,
unmoved by the happy holiday cheer
and the bargain slabs of ice cold beer.
He wakes when the selfish voice is broken.
Where equality and embrace are spoken.
Where the lonely do not sit alone.
And His gift of life is taken home.

Why don't you tell me that?

Be Different

Be different with me, that's OK.
Do things in your own funny way.
I'll applaud before God your right
To laugh when it's smart to be quiet
For there in your madness I see
Uniqueness, that's beauty to me.

Tutankhamun Exhibition: Melbourne

A hot Melbourne day,
tram lines shimmer in bitumen.
Pubs bulge a thirsty crowd
and old ladies melt in the Mall.

At Melbourne Museum, air-conditioned cool.
The Valley of Kings sits quiet in half light.
A silent escalator glides down hill
from the ticket booth to the tomb.
Zigzag lines of shufflers vanish into the desert
behind double doors.
The Nile Valley is at peace.

Ticketed pilgrims sharing body odour,
cheap perfume, and frustration,
slowly jostle to the sarcophagus.
Daytime night and dark corners
sprinkled with Hollywood
almost carries the illusion.
The tomb, cunningly crafted in fibreboard,
a shade short of spooky.

Thirteen-twenty-three BC chariot, as new.
Tables and chairs with millennial longevity.
Gold jewellery, handcrafted by an Egyptian genius,
all required for the great after journey
to Melbourne.

Pushing past polished glass, schoolkids
in daggy blazers, hemmed with grey ribbon,
circle in herds.
Boys pushing against girls
like stags in rut.
The girls giggle notes into folders,
loving the education
and living the moment.

The young Pharaoh, ignoring the tedium,
sleeps on.

Leaving Home

Leaving home
was not hard for me,
no handcuffs
chained my wrists.
I was running.
Adrenalin
pumping me up
like a junkie.
Everything good
was everywhere else.
I was a fish
grabbing the bait and running
for deep water.
The hook of home
had not then
turned my head.

Universe, Ants, and Loving God

The Universe and the ants
are marching in the Mall,
waving banners, chanting,
demanding their heritage
gifted to them
from beyond Dreamtime.
They seek a nod to their existence
being by thought
and plan.

Refusing to be splattered remnants
of the Big Bang.
When nothing became something
accidently.
Chaos
exploding outward into perfection,
like a mindless prank
in the school lab
that blew the building apart
creating a new school on the way down
with perfect class sizes,
balanced teacher to student ratios
and harmony in the corridors.

They march through the Mall
across the intersection
and vanish into tomorrow.
Chanting 'We were crafted
by the hand of the unimaginable,
beyond reach of dreaming minds
and the hard steel of mathematics.
We shout
with the voice of the invisible,
things that are clearly seen.

This is how we love God.'

Healing a Promise

She fell
into the arms of her shadow
and broke her promise
to take the kids to the zoo.

As gentle as a thought
she twisted down.
Arms outstretched to catch
her silhouette of softness.
It withdrew and she fell through,
tobogganing down the incline,
face forward.

One thoughtless step.
One unguarded commitment,
and her day went arse up.

Her pain screamed into the hollows
of the street.
Her face crinkled like newspaper.
She snapped, as if with the wave of a wand,
into the foetal position.

Fibula pieces thumped a base beat
through her head.

It took six weeks
to turn it into a melody.
Six weeks before she could walk again,
with her shadow, in the sun.

Now, you can hear her laughter
rattling with pots in the kitchen.

But the kids still whinge.
They skulk around the house
carrying a verbal limp
while kicking the zoo in front of them.

Fire of Silence

Under a blanket, a child
trembles, too afraid to cry.

Betrayal had come smiling,
in the polished shell of trust,
in the corrupt caresses of love.

Innocence was shredded.
Childhood thrown from its warm bed
onto a cold floor of shame.

The child speaks. Using silence.
Pleads behind empty eyes. A limp smile,
the band-aid on smouldering anger.

In a different place,
in a decade's time, the embers
are razor cuts, a bushfire
wintered in forest peat, flaring
into ice, drunkenness, addictions
that cool the frenzy

for a day.

A child. Under a blanket, trembling,
Too afraid to cry. Furious
for love stolen.

The silence speaks.
'You didn't listen,' it says.
'I'm loudest when there's pain.'

Escape

In my mind there is a chair.
On rainy days I wander there
and sit
with my back to the wind.
Nothing blows out
Nothing blows in.

When showers bend my outlook down
and leave me bogged in heavy ground,
I sit
in my mind unaware.
Dozing in my hiding chair.

Loving and Loathing

For my dearest clichés

Like children leaving home,
taking a piece of my heart,
clichés depart the haven
I have composed for them.

Those dear friends that offered
themselves as surrogates
to ease the tangled concentration
threshing in my mind.

They were compliant workers,
dressed in the mannerisms
and habits of bards, long dead.
They carelessly filled the potholes
along my poetic path
with sand.

Laughing larrikins, ready to munch
and guzzle the sweet images
brewing in the cellars of my
solitude.

Hangers–on intruding into personal
moments. Embarrassing each new beauty
I embraced by pissing on the leg
of originality.

Those lazy layabouts lounged
in my favourite chair
and created clutter wherever
they slumped themselves down.

I've waved them goodbye.
There's no going back.

… But I still leave a key
hidden under my mat.

Black and White Things

Things are black and white to me,
no shades of grey in what I see.
Right or wrong, up or down,
nicely squared, nothing round.
Nothing tapered, nothing new.
No need to weigh up points of view.
In confidence I stand aloof,
for as I see it, so is truth.

I disregard what people say,
unless they lean and bend my way.
No room for friends who disagree,
for even God agrees with me.

Acidic jibes and stereotypes
set my knowing mind to flight.
I proclaim to one and all
who falls short
and who stands tall.

Migrant influx uncontrolled,
adding thousands to the dole.
Upon the hot coals that I rake
Gays and Abos slowly bake.

All who stand outside my lines
will have their history redefined.
For only chosen colours grow
within the paddocks that I sow.

Late Onset Intelligence

Late onset intelligence came with arthritis
and revealed a three-course dinner
that should have been eaten young.

Primary school was the entrée,
a pleasant nibble at life.
The promise of a banquet
prepared in hungry minds.
But I was always a picky eater.

The soup of high school
was played with and left
half eaten.
It came with a roll
that was thrown at the teacher
and laughed about.

When the meat and veggies of university
was served, I wasn't at the table.
Mum kept telling me it was there
but I was hungry for other things.

My young heart desired the fast food of fun.
Instant sugar hits in the back of Dad's car,
Molly's romantic moaning, whispers of love.
Condensation trickling down windows,
leaching vitamins and minerals
from graduation day.

By twenty-one,
I was lip-sharing reefers
with mindless mates.
Group coughing.
All pockets emptied for a six-pack.
Intoxicated bragging trailing off
towards the pension.

Tomorrow sat on the table growing mould.

Now I'm hungry.

www.ingramcontent.com/pod-product-compliance
Lightning Source LLC
Chambersburg PA
CBHW070929080526
44589CB00013B/1449